THE MALTESE ISLANDS
FROM THE AIR

PHOTOGRAPHS BY JONATHAN BEACOM

TEXT BY GEOFFREY AQUILINA ROSS

PROUD
PUBLISHING
LIMITED

THE PHOTOGRAPHER DEDICATES THIS BOOK

TO HIS WIFE GLORYA AND SON JULIAN

© Text: Geoffrey Aquilina Ross

© Photography: Jonathan Beacom

Design: Ramon Micallef at Pulp Communications

Pre-Press, Printing and Binding: Gutenberg Press Limited, Malta.

ISBN: 99932-56-00-5

THE MALTESE ISLANDS
FROM THE AIR

FOREWORD

When Jonathan Beacom's aerial photographs of the Maltese Islands were first published in a book, the Islands were entering a decade of change. Those were the days before considerable investment was made in tourism, days when de luxe hotels were still being established and only a few cruise liners made the Grand Harbour their regular port of call. In this new edition, the book acknowledges the recent changes but, with its magnificent collection of images seen through the lens of a professional camera, it is also a celebration of Islands that have a unique place in history. After a superb study of the city of Valletta built by the Knights after the Great Siege of 1565, the photographic journey begins. The Grand Harbour is here too, so are the mediaeval city of Mdina, the distinctive landscapes that always seem to surprise visitors and the extraordinary Neolithic temples that were erected around 3500BC by the Islands' first settlers, a thousand years before the first pyramid in Egypt. The island of Gozo with its Citadel at the centre of the capital, Victoria, is here and so is the tiny sun-drenched island of Comino with its Blue Lagoon. This aerial odyssey records the archipelago as it is now, seen from above.

PROUD
PUBLISHING
LIMITED

CONTENTS

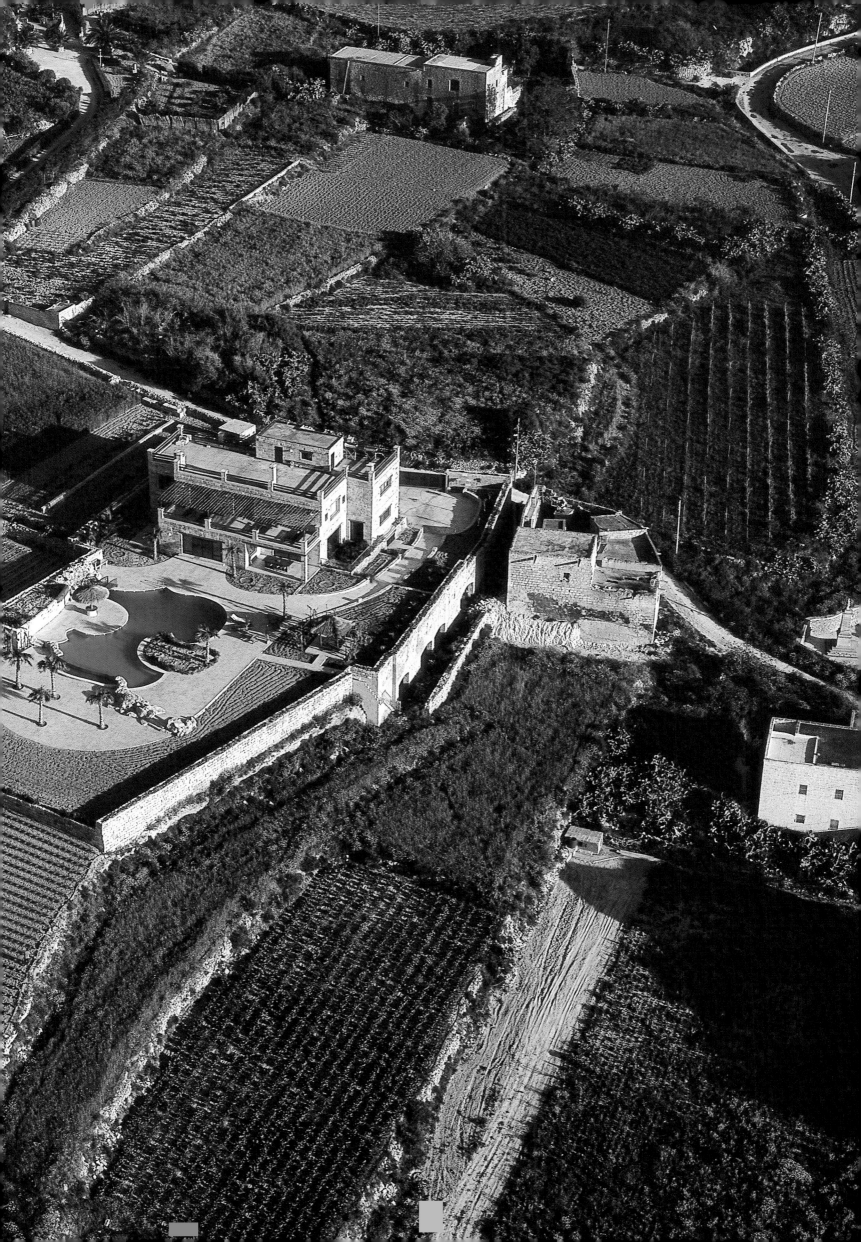

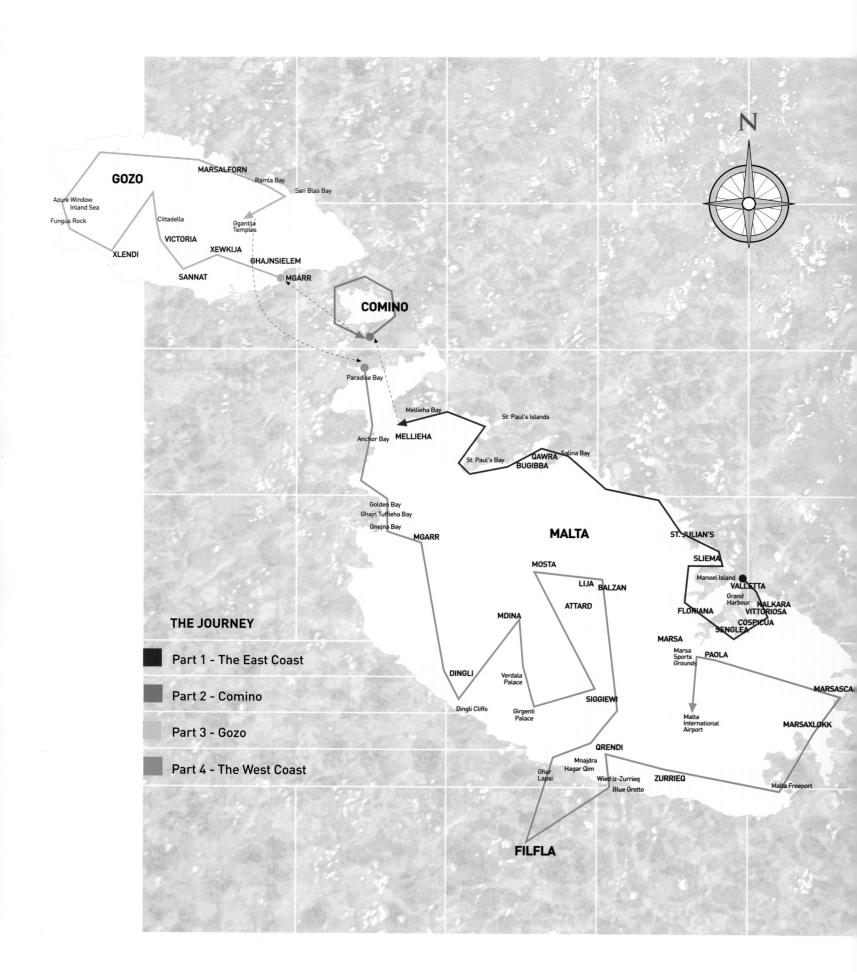

GOZO

Azure Window
Inland Sea

Fungus Rock

MARSALFORN

Ramla Bay

San Blas Bay

Cittadella

Ggantija
Temples

VICTORIA

XLENDI

XEWKIJA

SANNAT

GHAJNSIELEM

MGARR

COMINO

Paradise Bay

Mellieha Bay

St. Paul's Islands

Anchor Bay

MELLIEHA

St. Paul's Bay

Salina Bay

QAWRA

BUGIBBA

Golden Bay
Ghajn Tuffieha Bay

Gnejna Bay

MALTA

ST. JULIAN'S

MGARR

SLIEMA

MOSTA

LIJA

BALZAN

Manoel Island

VALLETTA

ATTARD

Grand
Harbour

KALKARA

MDINA

FLORIANA

VITTORIOSA

COSPICUA

SENGLEA

MARSA

THE JOURNEY

Marsa
Sports
Grounds

PAOLA

DINGLI

Verdala
Palace

SIGGIEWI

MARSASCA

Malta
International
Airport

MARSAXLOKK

Dingli Cliffs

Girgenti
Palace

- Part 1 - The East Coast

- Part 2 - Comino

- Part 3 - Gozo

- Part 4 - The West Coast

QRENDI

Mnajdra
Hagar Qim

Ghar
Lapsi

Wied iz-Zurrieq

ZURRIEQ

Blue Grotto

Malta Freeport

FILFLA

N

It is with a mixture of both amusement and exasperation when travelling the world that we Maltese often find ourselves explaining where the Islands are and what language we speak. Are the Islands Spanish, they often ask, because they assume we are alongside Majorca. Or maybe Greek – because on the map we seem to be close to Cyprus.

When we consider just how famous Malta has been in history, from the days of the Knights of the Order of St John of Jerusalem who to this day are known as the Knights of Malta, through to the magnificent heroism of the Islanders and the Allied forces stationed here in World War II, we fondly believe that everyone knows who and where we are. Perhaps, with our national airline, Air Malta, taking its place alongside far larger world carriers at international airports and our red-and-white national flag flying at the headquarters of the United Nations and the European Union, the questions are soon going to cease.

But of course, it is a fact. In spite of our long history, the Maltese Islands are still largely unknown. They are tiny; the total land area adds up to around 316 sq.km. And while they are in the Mediterranean Sea, they are near neither Spain nor Greece. We are at the very heart of the Mediterranean, midway between the Straits of Gibraltar and Egypt, with Sicily to the north and Libya on the coast of North Africa, directly south. Our language – because we have our own ancient language – is *Malti*, a language with Semitic roots and words borrowed from English and Italian.

The first settlers are believed to have arrived on Malta around 5000BC. Before that there may have been occasional visitors hunting wild game but it was not until animal husbandry and farming

VALLETTA

⌃ The Portes des Bombes gate on the outskirts of Floriana was originally erected in the 17th century as the entrance through a new outer ring of defensive walls outside Valletta. The entrance was a simple arched gate but, as the suburb of Floriana developed, so the gate was ornamented. During the Islands' British period, a second matching arch was added and two wide roadways were cut through the walls on either side to allow for increased road traffic.

❯ From above Marsamxett Harbour, the fortifications of Valletta and the Three Cities across the Grand Harbour show how forbidding and impregnable they would have seemed when first constructed by the Knights. Seen from the sea, as many travellers and mariners see the harbour, the strength of the towering stone bastions and ramparts is unquestionable. Boat excursions tour the harbours daily.

Surrounded by city buildings, St John's Co-Cathedral is one of the city's greatest treasures. Behind its plain façade is superb splendour and opulence. One of the first buildings to be completed by the Order of St John in their new city, it was consecrated as their conventual-church in 1578, but as each Knight endowed it with money or artifacts, so the church grew in importance. Its painted vault with superb frescoes by Mattia Preti, its richly decorated marble high altar and its colourful tapestry of memorial slabs that make up the floor proclaim the cathedral to be one of the finest in the world. St John's was declared a cathedral in 1816 by Pope Pius VII.

The Auberge de Castille is considered the finest example of Baroque architecture in Valletta. Originally designed as a Palace for the Grand Master, it was taken over in 1741 by Grand Master Manoel Pinto de Fonseca and designated the Auberge de Castile et Leon, the auberge of the knights of Spain and Portugal. It is now the Office of the Prime Minister.

On the weekend before Lent begins, from Friday until Ash Wednesday, carnival takes to the streets of Valletta. Every afternoon, as crowds line the pavements of Republic Street, groups of dancers and giant grotesques form a parade and stroll slowly and noisily, accompanied by music, towards Freedom Square. Everyone in the parade first makes an appearance in Palace Square outside the Palace of the Grand Masters, then sets off to the square where all the carnival groups, both local and foreign, dance and entertain the festive crowd. It is a relaxed, family occasion with many young children in the audience dressed in carnival costume. On the final day prizes are awarded to the best groups of dancers and to the teams making the most amusing towering grotesques and carnival floats.

GRAND HARBOUR

WHERE HISTORY WAS CREATED

For many centuries the fame of the Maltese Islands centred on the Grand Harbour. From the moment the nations dwelling on the coastlines of the Mediterranean started trading, this great deep-water port became the focus of travel, trading and power. Rich Phoenician merchants were based here from around 700BC until the Islands were lost to the Carthaginians in 550BC. As each nation conquered, so the harbour grew in importance and when the Order of St John was offered the Islands as its new home by King Charles I of Spain, it was the harbour that convinced the knights that the Islands were a suitable base, not the land which they considered barren and unproductive. However, in those times whoever controlled the harbour, controlled the centre of the Mediterranean Sea, and this strategic reason for owning the Islands continued even until World War II when aerial domination began to take over from sea power.

Today, with its fractured breakwaters and the historic forts at its entrance, the harbour is no longer a warlike base but an important port of call for international cruise ships and passenger ferries as well as for cargo vessels and for ships requiring repair and maintenance in the dockyards. Facing Senglea, historic Fort St Angelo now watches over a yacht marina instead of warships.

Fort St Angelo, once the fortress of the Knights and then headquarters of the British navy for two centuries, remains a remarkable historical site as it stands proudly overlooking the great harbour. Across the narrow Dockyard Creek is the town of Senglea, so badly damaged in World War II but now a thriving town.

French Creek, between the Senglea promontory and Kordin, is busy with ship repair and ship building facilities. The dockyards have capacity to service giant tankers as well as some of the world's finest liners.

The superb Grand Harbour with its fortresses and bastion walls that were erected in the days of the Knights, is now an important port of call for cruise liners and super-yachts. Passengers land here daily in order to see the city of Valletta and the Islands' historical sites. It is also a working port where cargo vessels unload their goods and ships and tankers enter the dockyards for repair and refit. A daily catamaran service runs from the quays here to Sicily.

Many of the world's finest cruise ships call in at the Grand Harbour during tours of the Mediterranean, dwarfing the historic fortifications built by the Knights as they lie alongside the quays. For many passengers this is the point of embarkation where their cruises begin; for others this is the opportunity for touring the Island. The QE2 makes a majestic appearance here while on world tours.

MARSAMXETT HARBOUR

YACHT MARINAS AND QUAYS FOR DAY-CRUISE BOATS

The days when Marsamxett Harbour was alive with warships are long gone. Today the harbour's creeks are busy with pleasure craft, with day-cruise boats ready to tour the Islands' coastline and with the bustling, serviced marinas that accommodate both large and small yachts. Facing Valletta is the resort town of Sliema with its selection of hotels, shops and restaurants and, at the centre of the harbour, is Manoel Island that was once a naval fortress and is now gradually being developed into a residential area. Both the historical traces of the Order of St John's Fort Manoel and the tiny island's renowned boatyard that is considered to have the best yacht slip facilities in the central Mediterranean will continue to give this small island its distinction.

SLIEMA
THE RESORT TOWN

Until the late 19th century Sliema was a hamlet where fishermen and their families lived. But as Maltese families became more wealthy, so they looked for new homes away from the narrow confines of Valletta. While the city itself had to be easily accessible for work and commerce, what the families required was a seaside location where they could establish elegant houses that would be cool enough for them to enjoy the hot summer months. Gradually, as houses were built, the Islands' prime residential town came into being and since then it has flourished and expanded to such an extent that, while it remains a residential town, its excellent location has ensured that it has also developed into a flourishing holiday resort.

There are a variety of excellent hotels, restaurants and cafès and, along the promenade that leads to the entertainments district of St Julian's, numbers of tall expensive apartment buildings with expansive sea views. Language schools teaching English to foreign students flourish, so do shops, stores and supermarkets that cater to locals and visitors alike. A ferry service to Valletta runs from the harbour waterfront alongside the cruise boats that set out daily to tour the Islands.

SLIEMA

The gracious promenade leading from the harbour waterfront follows the rugged coastline to St Julian's and Paceville. It is on this pale-coloured rock shoreline that families gather to enjoy the sunshine, picnicking and swimming in the clear, blue sea. While children can snorkle in safety, waterpolo teams compete in club competitions that are as avidly followed as the national soccer leagues. In the hot summer months families gather on the popular stretches of beach until the cooler late hours.

ST JULIAN'S
RESTAURANTS, CAFÉS AND LATE NIGHTS

As the promenade leaves Sliema, so it passes through Balluta Bay with its own waterpolo clubs to reach St Julian's which, with neighbouring Paceville, has developed into the island's great entertainments district. There are a wide variety of restaurants and cafés with open air, waterfront views here as well as late night venues and cinemas. Small hotels favoured by families and young holidaymakers sit alongside five-star de luxe hotels with their private lidos. Overlooking the attractive Portomaso marina edged with fine apartments is the island's first high-rise office building. On the promontory that separates St Julian's from neighbouring St George's Bay, is an elegant casino in a charming summer palace that was once the home of a Marquis.

The Portomaso Marina on the edge of St Julian's offers shelter to some of the finest boats and yachts in the Mediterranean. Elegant apartments, a de luxe hotel and a number of restaurants overlook its car-free promenade. Fine hotels in this district have their own lidos on the rocky coastline.

St George's Bay, in a tranquil setting a few minutes away from the bustle of St Julian's and Paceville, has an excellent selection of de luxe hotels, facing the bay and the open sea, each one with fine restaurants and cafés as well as spas and waterside lidos. It is a perfect location for a relaxed holiday.

SALINA BAY & QAWRA

ANCIENT SALT PANS AND MODERN HOTELS

The shallow tranquil waters of Salina's creek have been used to produce commercial quantities of natural sea salt in a series of man-made shallow ponds for many decades. Fish farms have been introduced nearby.

Along the coast road leading to Salina a large modern hotel with sea and country views dominates the landscape while at Qawra, a growing resort area, similar hotels nestling among the apartment buildings have private lidos and excellent watersport facilities.

ST PAUL'S BAY

WHERE THE SAINT WAS SHIPWRECKED

The statue of St Paul was erected on St Paul's Island in 1845. The saint was shipwrecked on this rocky promontory in AD 60 on his way for trial in Rome. Underwater a short distance away is a statue of Christ placed there with a blessing from Pope John Paul II during a visit to the island in 1990.

> *The Bugibba waterfront in St Paul's Bay is busy for most of the year. Day cruises set off from here for tours of the Islands and many family boats are anchored in the sheltered calm of the bay. Bugibba is a bustling resort with a wide selection of inexpensive hotels, restaurants, cafés and bars.*

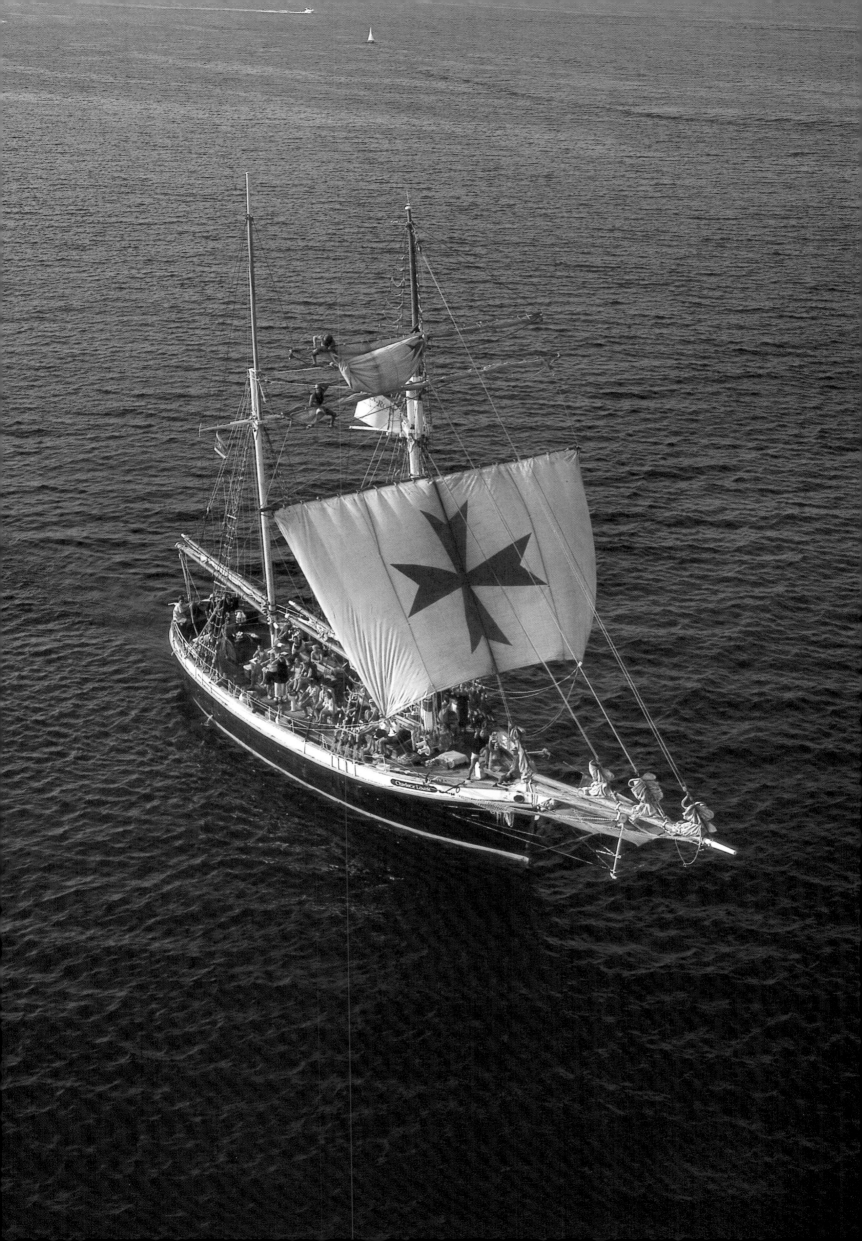

The sea around the Maltese Islands is deep, clear and blue. In the summer months there is nothing more pleasurable than taking the day out, swimming and picnicking. Or out on a boat, whether it is a traditional brightly coloured Maltese luzzu or one of the many day cruise boats that offer tours to secluded bays or around the Islands.

MELLIEHA BAY

AND THE BEACH OF GHADIRA

Below the village of Mellieha, with the parish church of the Nativity of Our Lady at its centre, is Malta's largest sandy beach, Ghadira. This attractive wide sweep of beach with its excellent facilities and watersports is very popular, especially with young families. Behind the sands is a marshy nature reserve teeming with migratory bird life and on the hillside where the road leads northwards to Gozo is St Agatha's Tower giving extra distinction to the bay. Erected in 1649 by the Order of St John, it is known to all as the Red Tower because of its colour.

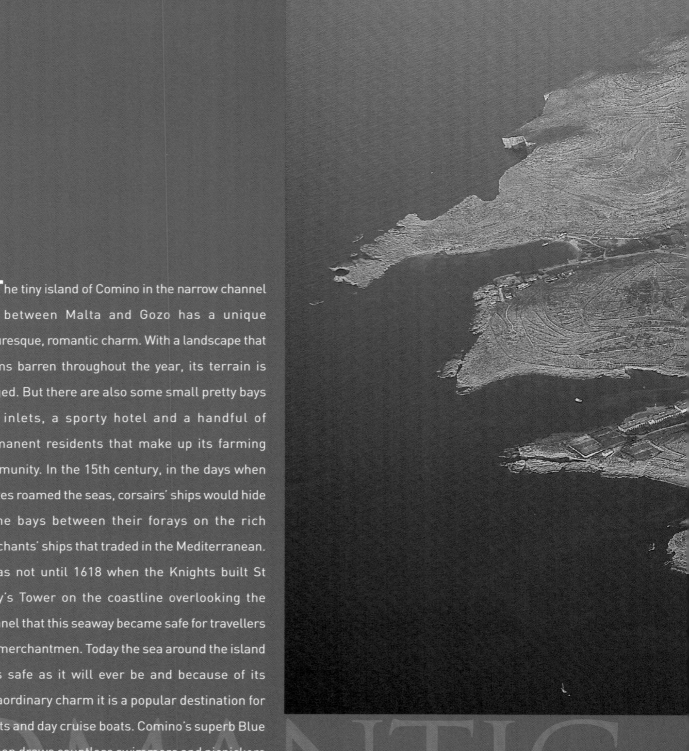

The tiny island of Comino in the narrow channel between Malta and Gozo has a unique picturesque, romantic charm. With a landscape that seems barren throughout the year, its terrain is rugged. But there are also some small pretty bays and inlets, a sporty hotel and a handful of permanent residents that make up its farming community. In the 15th century, in the days when pirates roamed the seas, corsairs' ships would hide in the bays between their forays on the rich merchants' ships that traded in the Mediterranean. It was not until 1618 when the Knights built St Mary's Tower on the coastline overlooking the channel that this seaway became safe for travellers and merchantmen. Today the sea around the island is as safe as it will ever be and because of its extraordinary charm it is a popular destination for yachts and day cruise boats. Comino's superb Blue Lagoon draws countless swimmers and picnickers into its delightful turquoise waters. Inlets around the coastline of Comino, and the even smaller outcrop of rock called Cominotto that edges the Blue Lagoon, are excellent creeks for day cruise boats with their enthusiastic passengers. The clear sea is perfect.

ROMANTICA

ND RUGGED

St Mary's Tower was built in 1618 on the high ground overlooking the island and its bays as well as the shipping routes north of Malta. Sentries stationed on its flat-topped roof could warn the city of Valletta by means of bonfires of an enemy fleet approaching or of a pirate ship sheltering in the nearby bays. It was only after the tower was built that pirates stopped sheltering in Comino's bays.

In the channel between Malta and Gozo, the island of Comino makes an excellent destination for yachts of all sizes. It features in many of the Islands' annual yacht races.

On the edge of the island's rugged landscape facing Gozo, the small bays of San Niklaw and Santa Marija have a simple, romantic charm. To capture the mood, the island's hotel with its seclusion and wide selection of sea sports offers an idyllic escape.

GOZO

ISLAND

The island of Gozo has shared Malta's history though, for the most part, on a smaller scale. While the temples of *Ġgantija* outside Xaghra rival *Haġar Qim* and *Mnajdra* in Malta, the Knights of the Order of St John only came here in small numbers and so bequeathed little of the wealth of glorious architecture that would so dramatically enhance Malta. In fact, although the Knights came to establish a ring of defensive towers around the island to act as protection should the Ottoman forces attack, their construction of the bastion walls around the Citadel in Rabat at the centre of Gozo was initially carried out in order to protect the island's small rural communities from the corsairs who raided the island to kidnap the inhabitants. In 1551 thousands of inhabitants were carried off in one raid and after this, until 1637, all Gozitans were bound by law to sleep in the Citadel for their own protection. During the British era Rabat was renamed Victoria in honour of the Queen's jubilee and, later, its tiny airfield played an important part in the defence of the Islands in World War II.

In Gozo traditions last and family values are

high. Its islanders have always remained faithful to the land and farms flourish – each season the crops seem temptingly rich and bountiful.

Even though the island is small, the landscape can be breathtaking with its rugged hills and green valleys watered by natural springs. While tourism advances and more development takes place, the countryside still retains an unspoiled charm.

Gozo is a wonderful low key place for a holiday. There are excellent hotels and restaurants and some delightful beaches to entice the visitor.

CHARM

F CHARM

MĠARR HARBOUR

GATEWAY TO THE ISLAND

Mgarr is the island's only port, an attractive working harbour permanently busy with commercial traffic as well as its small fishing fleet and a well-serviced yacht marina. As all passenger and car ferry services linked to Malta's northern port of Cirkewwa sail from its quays, Mgarr is where most visitors first step ashore. Overlooking the tiny bay are two elegant, modern hotels and a neo-Gothic church built in the late-19th century. In the creek old boathouses once used by fishermen have been transformed into excellent fish restaurants.

THREE CHURCHES

GĦAJNSIELEM, XEWKIJA AND SANNAT

Every village and town has a parish church that distinguishes it from its neighbours. At Għajnsielem the tall neo-Gothic church dedicated to Madonna of Loreto has one of the few spires on the Islands while at Xewkija the dome of St John the Baptist is reputed to be the third largest unsupported dome in the world. The more modest church of St Margaret at Sannat sits at the crossroads that lead to the spectacular cliffs at Ta' Cenc.

THE CITADEL
SURVEYING THE COUNTRYSIDE

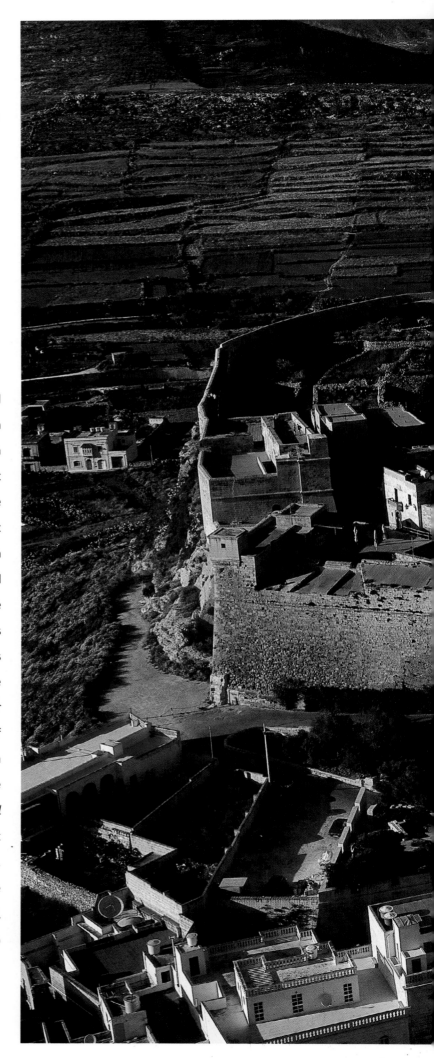

Surrounded by great walls, the Citadel (*il-Kastell*) overlooks the island capital, Victoria. The hill on which it stands was always considered an excellent defensive position for times of war, but it was not until the early-17th century that the Order of St John built the bastion walls that surround it in order to protect the population from being snatched by corsairs who raided the island in order to sell the inhabitants as slaves on the Barbary Coast. In 1551 thousands of inhabitants were carried·off in one raid so, until the Knights rid the sea of pirates in 1637, all Gozitans were required by law to sleep in the Citadel for their own protection. Within its walls today is a gem of a small early-18th century cathedral. Money ran out during its construction so a magnificent dome was never completed. However a *trompe l'oeil* painting (1739) successfully disguises this fact when viewed from inside the charming church. Among the other buildings in the Citadel are the museums of Folklore, Archeology and Natural History. Views from the ramparts offer superb panoramas of Gozo's remarkable landscape.

IN THE COUNTRYSIDE

TRANQUILLITY AND THE TA' PINU SANCTUARY

The historic Citadel above the island's capital, Victoria, looks as it has done for centuries, mysterious and impregnable.

◀ *The hilltop village of Zebbug with its parish church at its centre stretches along a narrow ridge bordered by fertile valleys.*

▶ *It was in 1883 that a local peasant woman in a small chapel in the tranquil valley outside Ghammar heard the voice of the Virgin. A friend confided that he too had heard the voice, and together they prayed for his critically ill mother. His mother recovered. As word spread so miracle cures multiplied and in the 1920s it was decided to build a church to accommodate the numbers of pilgrims visiting the shrine. The original chapel was incorporated into the new neo-Romanesque church, behind the altar. To one side, in a corridor, is a poignant display of crutches, splints and baby clothes that bear witness to other miracle cures after prayer here. On the hillside facing the shrine is the Way of the Cross that forms part of the Easter calendar.*

XLENDI

EDGED BY CLIFFS

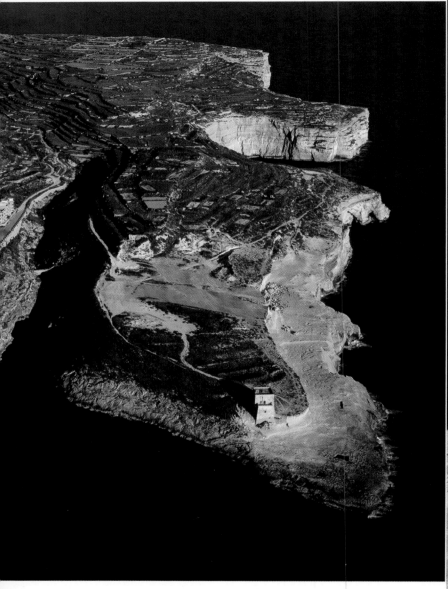

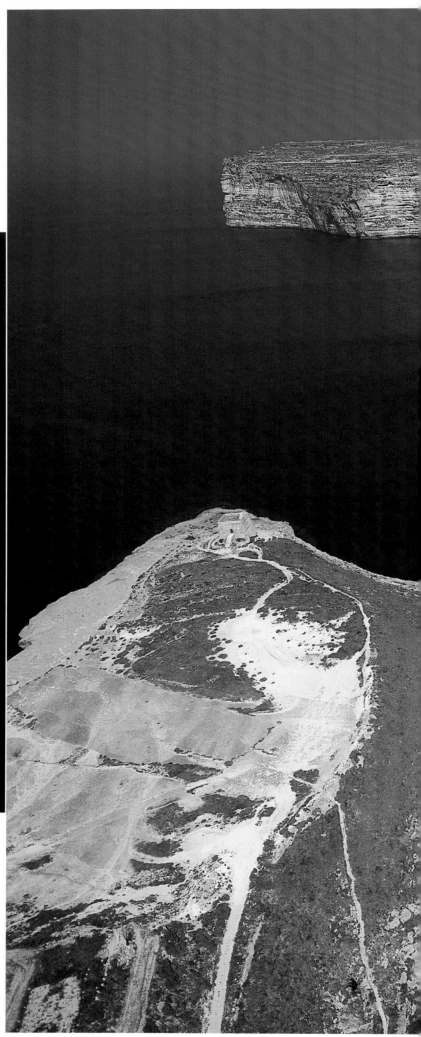

A tiny inlet protected by great cliffs leads in to Xlendi, the smaller of Gozo's two resorts. Behind its narrow strip of sand covered shoreline there are hotels, a selection of restaurants and bars, and some souvenir shops. Brightly painted fishing boats anchor in its sheltered creek. New development is confined to one hillside.

DWEJRA

WITH FUNGUS ROCK AND THE INLAND SEA

On the coast outside the village San Lawrenz is Dwejra with its spectacular and dramatic landscape. The bay is deep with indigo blue sea and, standing tall at its entrance, is Fungus Rock where a fungus much prized by the Knights for medicinal purposes was once said to grow. Overlooking Dwejra is Qawra watchtower built in 1651 to prevent pirates sheltering in the secluded bay.

The Inland Sea was formed in ancient times when the roof of a giant cave collapsed and sea poured in through a narrow fissure in the cliffs. The shallow crater has a number of boathouses and a small jetty from which visitors can take boat trips through the tunnel to the sea outside to view the towering cliffs and the extraordinary Azure Window archway that juts out from the land.

◀ *The salt pans cut into the limestone rock outside Qbajjar have been producing great quantities of natural sea salt since Roman times. The pans are inherited, handed down through generations of families.*

▶ *Adding delightful imagery to the slight promontory that separates Qbajjar from Xwieni Bay is a weathered limestone and clay mound known as 'Qolla l-Bajda' (an earthenware jar used for wine) and a fortress built in 1620, during the times of the Knights.*

MARSALFORN

RELAXED RESORT

Once a fishing village, Marsalforn has grown into Gozo's largest resort. But it remains casual and relaxed, reflecting the island's way of life. Along its promenade are restaurants and cafés and a tiny man-made harbour to shelter fishing boats.

After a petition by sportsmen and farmers in 1901, a wooden cross was placed on the brow of the conical hill outside Marsalforn. Then in 1904, to commemorate a religious event, a stone statue of Is-Salvatur replaced the cross. This withered, so in November 1960 the monument was replaced by one in concrete, 11m high. However, in the 1990s, this was struck by lightning and collapsed and for some time Gozitans waited for calamity to follow. None did, so a replacement statue was made, this time in fiberglass. It should have better luck.

Near the tiny, pretty sandy beach of San Blas the Kortin Tower stands proudly on top of the rocky cliff. The tower, built by the Knights, is one of the many watchtowers that circle the Islands.

△ The *Ġgantija* temples are on the edge of the high ridge alongside the village of Xaghra. Built in the early years of the Temple Period, between 3600-2500BC, they are the best preserved temples on the Maltese Islands. Their monumental walls stand, unrestored, at more than 6m.

Outside Nadur, the two red sand beaches of Gozo offer superb days by the sea in the summer months. Unspoiled Ramla at the end of a fertile valley has just a few cafés by its parking area, but not much more by way of facilities. This long sweep of beach with a tiny statue of the Virgin facing the sea has a gentle slope into the shallows and is a haven for families. San Blas is like a much smaller and prettier Ramla but is reached only by a steep footpath suitable for young and fit picnickers. There are no commercial facilities here.

ON THE WESTERN COAST

Turning southwards again, the flight crosses the sea to continue along Malta's western coastline, over the golden beaches of Paradise Bay, Ghajn Tuffieha and Golden Bay before hovering above the dramatic rocky heights of Dingli Cliffs with the tiny rock island nature reserve that is Filfla in its solitary position out to sea. Inland there is the tiny farming village of Mgarr with its towering parish church and Mdina, the magnificent mediaeval walled city that is still lived in today, with its splendid cathedral and, in its narrow winding streets, a wonderful mixture of palaces, convents, restaurants, cafés, de luxe hotel and theatrical presentations that inform visitors of the city's historical roots.

As the journey continues so there are the island's distinctive villages and the two remarkable prehistoric temples of *Hagar Qim* and *Mnajdra* which were erected around 3600BC, nearly 1000 years before the first pyramid in Egypt.

The picturesque inlet of Wied iz-Zurrieq is here too, so are the quarries where stone from which Malta's houses are built is taken from the ground, and the Malta Freeport that so successfully handles the transshipment of goods from all over the world. The odyssey finally ends at Malta International Airport, the Islands' airport that greets visitors to the Maltese Islands and acts as an important hub for passengers travelling across the Mediterranean to far away destinations.

The photographic record of the Maltese Islands is complete.

EY CONTINUES

EY CONT

PARADISE BAY

FAMILY FAVOURITE

In its picturesque location surrounded by rugged cliffs on the northern tip of Malta near Cirkewwa, Paradise Bay with its stretch of sand and excellent beach facilities is a family favourite. The setting is pretty, the sea is crystal clear.

↖ *Popeye Village alongside Anchor Bay was built as the Sweethaven set for the 1980 Robin Williams movie* Popeye *and been preserved as a tourist attraction with the addition of an amusement park. Children love it.*

→ *Sea, sun and sand: three essential ingredients for a wonderful summer. The Islands' sandy beaches offer the whole family the greatest potential for wonderful holidays and summertime outings.*

FAMILY FUN

POPEYE VILLAGE AND WELCOMING SEA

GOLDEN BAY
FAMILY BEACH

With the small Lascaris watchtower built by the Knights overlooking the beach, Golden Bay is a popular family summer destination, especially at weekends. It is an attractive beach with a wide range of facilities.

GHAJN TUFFIEHA

DRAMATICALLY ATTRACTIVE

Reached by a steep climb, Ghajn Tuffieha is visually more dramatic than neighbouring Golden Bay but, because of its difficult access, always less crowded. The sand is ideal for children so the beach is popular for family outings. Facilities are limited to a small café.

ĠNEJNA BAY

PICTURESQUE BEACH

Another great, scenic bay, with boathouses to one side, a secluded cream-coloured rock for sunworshipers and simple beach facilities on the sands. At the end of a deep fertile valley, the setting of the bay is delightful.

MĠARR
FARMING COMMUNITY

The tall parish church of Santa Marija was built in the 1930s by donations from the parishioners. Many were so poor and had little money so, instead, to raise the required money for building the church they would bring produce like sacks of potatoes from the fields for the parish priest to sell in the market. Their *festa* is on 15 August.

> *The fertile countryside is made up of a patchwork of fields belonging to numerous farmers. In the summer months most fields lie fallow but as the seasons change so the produce becomes abundant. Crops like potatoes and onions form an important part of the Islands' exports. Although farm machinery is used, much of the work can only be carried out by hand because of the inaccessibility of the terraced fields.*

LANDSCAPE DRAMA

MTAĦLEB AND THE TOWERING CLIFFS

The dramatic cliffs of *Rdum tas-Sarġ* with the headland of *Ras ir-Raħeb* jutting out to sea make the coastline outside Mtaħleb spectacular. It is an area to explore and a favourite location for walkers in the winter and spring months.

The sheer cliffs on the western coastline create a superb dramatic landscape as they tower over the deep blue sea.

With the village of Dingli in the distance, the Dingli Cliffs at around 250m are the highest spot in Malta.

At Fawwara close to Siggiewi the little chapel of Tac-Cawla faces out to sea and the island of Filfla.

MDINA
WALLED MEDIAEVAL CITY

On high ground, this gracious mediaeval city is the old capital of the Islands. After the Order of St John had completed building Valletta they added to the bastions walls and ramparts of Mdina but rechristened it *Citta Vecchia*, the Old City, and moved all civil and legal life to the new capital. However Mdina remains a fine example of a mediaeval walled city and, with its fine cathedral, convents, palaces, cafés and restaurants, it is still alive today. There has always been a community on this prominent site and in AD60, in Roman times, St Paul preached here, converting many of the inhabitants to Christianity.

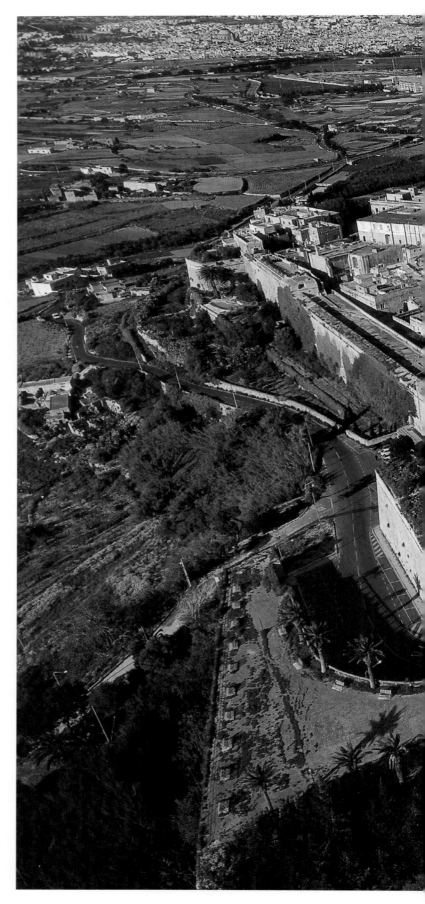

From the distance the cathedral majestically dominates Mdina and the surrounding countryside. It gives the gracious walled city its unique silhouette.

Mdina Cathedral dedicated to St Paul is believed to stand on the site of the house of the head man of the community, Publius, when St Paul visited Mdina in AD60. Publius became the saint's first Christian convert in Malta and later the first Bishop of Malta. In January 1693 an earthquake destroyed the original cathedral, but by 1702 an even greater one had risen from the ashes. Behind its Baroque façade lies a superb and wealthily decorated church.

From the tall ramparts and bastions walls of Mdina there are extensive panoramas of the countryside. Villages like Mosta are recognizable so too, in the distance, is the younger city of Valletta. Many of the patrician houses along the bastion walls have opened cafés and restaurants with excellent views.

VERDALA CASTLE
GRAND MASTER'S SUMMER PALACE

Built in 1586 as a summer residence for Grand Master Hugues de Verdalle, the retreat was designed to look like a traditional mediaeval keep surrounded by a dry moat. But although there are secret passages and a cell used for torture hidden in its walls, the castle was not designed to withstand attack. It was created as a comfortable home. The Grand Master hunted game in the *boschetto* woodland below (now Buskett Gardens). The castle is the President of Malta's summer retreat.

GIRGENTI

THE INQUISITOR'S SUMMER PALACE

A beautiful country house in a secluded position outside Siggiewi, the palace
was built in 1625 as the summer residence of the Inquisitor, Horatus Visconti.
With fine views along the fertile valley, the great house provided an elegant, airy
home far from the narrow confines of the Inquistor's offices in Vittoriosa. Today,
known as Girgenti, the building is used by the Prime Minister for official meetings.

Not far from Siggiewi on the hill known as *Is-Salib ta' l-Għolja* is the Laferla Cross erected alongside the hill's simple chapel by a generous benefactor. The hill has fine views over the countryside and so is a place for picnickers during the cooler months of the year. During Lent, before Easter Sunday, it becomes the focus of religious gatherings.

The great dome of the parish church in Mosta seems visible from almost any
vantage point on the island. Known to the parishioners as Santa Marija Assunta,
it is often referred to as the Rotunda or, simply, Mosta Dome. The foundations
were laid in 1833 but it took 28 years to complete due to complex domestic
problems, a cholera epidemic and the archbishop's refusal to bless the church
himself because it was round rather than in the traditional shape of a cross.
The unsupported dome was constructed without the use of scaffolding because
it was built over a smaller church already standing there.

MOSTA

THE GREAT DOME

The excellent workmanship erecting the dome was tested during World War II when a bomb pierced it, falling to the church floor and causing the congregation to flee. Miraculously it did not explode and only minimal damage was caused to the dome itself. The diffused bomb is on show in the church.

LIJA

ONE OF THE THREE VILLAGES

Lija, Attard and Balzan were once three distinctive neighbouring inland villages surrounded by countryside. As building development progressed, so each grew in size to touch its neighbours boundaries, yet somehow each retained its own individuality. Lija is distinguished by the wide Transfiguration Avenue lined with oleanders and decorative stone folly sweeping up to the imposing Baroque parish church of the Our Saviour, known as *is-Salvatur*, built in 1694.

Lija is famous for its *festa* on 6 August and the spectacular firework displays that draw the crowds.

FILFLA

ROCKY ISLAND SANCTUARY

The barren rock in the dark blue sea off the coast south of Siggiewi has been declared a nature reserve. Migratory birds rest here with Filfla's only other known residents, lizards, for company. It is believed that early man in the temples of *Mnajdra* and *Hagar Qim* revered the tiny island that seems to rise from the sea for its mystical powers.

MNAJDRA
NEOLITHIC TEMPLES

On high ground on the coastline facing the island of Filfla, the Neolithic temples of *Mnajdra* are in a sheltered position on the hillside below Malta's other important temples of *Hagar Qim*. Erected around 3500BC, these complex temples are formed with tall standing stones, many of which arch inwards and may therefore have supported a roof. The great stone slabs were moved around on large stone balls and then manoeuvered into holes in the ground with wooden spars. The three temples on the Maltese Islands are the oldest free-standing buildings in the world.

ĦAĠAR QIM

ERECTED AROUND 3500BC

The Islands' three Neolithic temples have been declared UNESCO World Heritage sites as there is nothing to match them anywhere in the world. It is believed the temples were used for religious ceremonies by early man and many important objects discovered during excavations are now housed in the National Museum of Archaeology in Valletta. At *Ħaġar Qim* the largest stone measures 7m and weighs around 20 tonnes.

WIED IŻ-ŻURRIEQ

FISHING BOATS AND THE BLUE GROTTO

This picturesque narrow inlet in the barren rocky coastline outside Zurrieq has been used by fishermen for many centuries. Their brightly coloured boats shelter in the creek or are pulled up the slipway for repair during winter months. Many of the fishermen's old houses have been turned into simple cafés and restaurants that serve fresh fish. Visitors can take boats from its slender quay to visit the Blue Grotto caves that burrow into the cliffs a short distance away.

AROUND QRENDI

LEGEND AND SUPERSTITION

The village of Qrendi is distinctive with the imposing church of St Mary at its centre. Near the church is the 16th century Cavalier Tower, the island's only octagonal tower where villagers sought refuge in times of danger and would rain down rocks and tar from its roof onto their attackers.

Il-Maqluba, close to the fields producing quantities of the islands' excellent potato crops, is an eerie hole with tangled vegetation about 50m deep. In Maltese 'Maqluba' means 'turned upside down'. God, it seems, was displeased with the sins of the villagers and tore away the ground under their feet, sending them down towards hell. A deep hole was formed. Legend says the place is cursed.

ŻURRIEQ

VILLAGE IN THE SOUTH

Close to the Neolithic temples and picturesque Wied iz-Zurrieq, the village's parish church dedicated to St Catherine of Alexandria dates back to 1632. A fine church, it was designed by its own parish priest and took 27 years to complete. It was also superbly decorated by Mattia Preti, the Italian Baroque artist who so superbly decorated St John's Co-Cathedral in Valletta.

ACKNOWLEDGEMENTS

The photographer thanks the many people who contributed to the making of this book.

He would especially like to express his gratitude to the following:

Armed Forces of Malta (AFM):

Brigadier Rupert Montanaro - Commander

Major Martin Sammut – for helicopter flight clearances

AFM Helicopter Squadron:

Major Ronnie Xuereb – Officer Commanding

Pilots: Capt. Anthony Zammit.   Sgt. Ivan Marmara

Civilian Fixed Wing Pilot: Karl Grech

Microlight Pilot: Major Alex Dalli (Island Microlight Club)

Geoffrey Aquilina Ross, not just for his informative and enlightening text but also for

painstakingly researching, editing and proofing the contents of this book.

Designer Ramon Micallef for the many, many hours enthusiastically spent on layout and design.

Andrew Muscat at Gutenberg Pre-Press Dept. who also dedicated many hours to the project.

Frank Spiteri and all his staff at Gutenberg Press.

The photo of the QE2 on page 44 by courtesy of Mifsud Brothers Limited.